A Cup of Grace... to Go

A Cup of Grace... to Go

What Jesus Might Say to Start Your Day

Anita M. Constance

ave maria press   Notre Dame, Indiana

www.avemariapress.com

International Standard Book Number: 0-87793-965-9
Cover and text design by Brian C. Conley
Printed and bound in the United States of America.

Library of Congress Cataloging-in-Publication Data
Constance, Anita M., 1945-
A cup of grace-- to go : what Jesus might say to start your day / Anita M. Constance.
     p. cm.
ISBN 0-87793-965-9 (pbk.)
     1.   Meditations.   2.   Bible. N.T. Gospels--Meditations. 3. Catholic Church--Prayer-books and devotions--English. I. Title.
BX2182.3 .C66 2002
242--dc21

                                        CIP
                                        2001005604

To
Anita M. Pierro, my grandmother,
and the Sisters at Saint Anne Villa,
Convent Station, New Jersey—
women who have made the ordinary extraordinary!

Indeed, the word of God is living and active,
sharper than any two-edged sword,
piercing until it divides soul from spirit, joints from marrow;
it is able to judge the thoughts and intentions of the heart.

—Hebrews 4:12

A Note to the Reader . . .

If you're like me, you look forward to that morning cup of coffee, tea, or other beverage to get you started each day. Fortified by this jump into life, we enter the race of our fast-paced world, often finding ourselves out the door with no more than a nod to God as we cross the threshold. We return home tired—the end of a long and active day. Again, God might be given a quick nod as we settle down for a good night's sleep. But is this enough?

A Cup of Grace . . . to Go addresses our prayer-thirst—as vital to our spirits as food to our bodies. This is simple prayer, heart-prayer that reflects upon the gospels and offers a surprising word from the author of "good news," Jesus Christ.

A suggestion: Take one cup at breakfast, stirred with the scriptures and companioned by the Word who is life.

Blessings for the journey!
Anita, SC

**AND JESUS SAID TO THEM, "FOLLOW ME. . . ." AND
IMMEDIATELY THEY LEFT THEIR NETS AND FOLLOWED HIM
(MK 1:17-18).**

Jesus, I wish I could abandon my plans as quickly. What did your apostles have that I don't? What made it so easy for them to drop everything and follow you? James and John were preparing their nets, probably making plans for the next day's fishing. Then you walk by, a total stranger, and that was that. Right on the spot, their lives were changed!

What happened to the theory that snap decisions are best avoided? It appears they cast away discernment as well as their nets. They even walked out on their father! Not a second glance. No guilt about not carrying on the family business. What impressed them about you that they could leave it all behind?

Jesus: Do you really want to know, or is it safer to protest and prod me with questions?

Follow me. Leave the past behind. Trust that others can take care of themselves.

Suggested Scripture:

MATTHEW 4:12-17
MARK 1:14-20
LUKE 4:14-15

**". . . [JESUS] COMMANDS EVEN THE UNCLEAN SPIRITS,
AND THEY OBEY HIM"
(MK 1:27).**

Jesus, I'd like a few words from you, too. Just one or two that would cast the lasting spell of healing over me. After all, you have the authority. You have the power to change what seems unchangeable—namely, me! I want to hear the words that will take away my unclean spirit— that one sin I can only whisper to you in the darkness. I've tried everything, but day after day, year after year, it shows up as inevitable as the dawn. I don't like it shining in the light of each new day. I want to wrap it in a shroud and bury it forever.

Jesus: I can heal your sin only when you stop hiding it. What you fear to reveal to the light can be freed from its darkness . . . when held in the gaze of my grace.

Suggested Scripture:

MARK 1:21-28
LUKE 4:31-37

SIMON'S MOTHER-IN-LAW LAY SICK WITH A FEVER. THEY IMMEDIATELY TOLD [JESUS] ABOUT HER (MK 1:30, NAB).

For me, Lord Jesus, you are often the last one to know. If something is bothering me or I am concerned about someone I love, I turn to myself as first resource in this need. When I exhaust that well, I begin to panic. "What will happen?" I ask myself. "How will things work out, if I can't work them out?" My spirit groans and grumbles within me. My heart heaves a sigh as I sink into worry and useless despair. Why do I have to go that far before I remember that you are God, not I?

I wish I had the faith of Peter and your first disciples. They knew to whom they should go. After all the miracles you have performed in my life, why am I still so crippled?

Jesus: Maybe the crutch you desire to throw away is still more comfortable than the freedom faith would provide. Miracles happen when you walk, however lame, toward me.

Suggested Scripture:

MATTHEW 8:14-17
MARK 1:29-39
LUKE 4:38-41

[JESUS] SAID TO HIM, "SEE THAT YOU TELL NO ONE ANYTHING, BUT GO, SHOW YOURSELF TO THE PRIEST AND OFFER FOR YOUR CLEANSING WHAT MOSES PRESCRIBED; THAT WILL BE PROOF FOR THEM"
(MK 1:44, NAB).

Here is where we are really different, Jesus. I like people to know my successes. If I do a good job, I want to shout it from the housetops. Why wouldn't *you*? It was leprosy, Jesus. You cured a man of leprosy! You restored him to society and to his family. It must have been a grand homecoming—and all because of you!

I envy your ability to do good and to move on. I prefer to revel in that good for a while. How do you know when enough is enough? How will I know when just the "good" is enough? After all, I'm only human.

Jesus: Exactly. Before you open the door to celebration, remember the One who made it possible for you.

Suggested Scripture:

MATTHEW 8:1-4
MARK 1:40-45
LUKE 5:12-16

A Cup of Grace:

Jesus, every time I read this story, I marvel at what great friends the paralytic had. Everyone values the treasure of friendship; I do. I know I can count on my friends, but today I wonder if I could entrust myself to them as completely as this man did.

You see, I can't imagine being carried by others for most of my life, or even for a part of it. I can't imagine never "doing" for my friends, always being cared for instead. Would I believe myself to be a worthy treasure for them? It seems the paralytic did, but would I know my value as well?

Jesus: The coin of friendship never changes its value, no matter the cost to you or to another.

Suggested Scripture:

MATTHEW 9:2-8
MARK 2:1-12
LUKE 5:17-26

12

> . . . MANY TAX COLLECTORS AND SINNERS WERE ALSO
> SITTING WITH JESUS AND HIS DISCIPLES. . . . WHEN THE
> SCRIBES OF THE PHARISEES SAW . . . THEY SAID TO HIS
> DISCIPLES, "WHY DOES HE EAT WITH
> TAX COLLECTORS AND SINNERS?"
> (MK 2:15-16).

Jesus, somewhere along the line we learned to be careful of our associations. Who spent time with us, whom we called friend were reflections of ourselves. This kind of thinking never entered your mind, though. For you, those with whom you ate, walked, and spoke were reflections of our God. You saw only brothers and sisters, so what others thought or said did not keep you from companionship. Concern drove your heart to feel their longing and fill their need. Who am I, then, to act at times so detached from the human family? Heal me from my blindness of heart and emptiness of soul, for these sins of the Pharisees are also "guests"—though not welcomed ones—at my table.

Jesus: Perhaps your guest list needs to be revised.

Suggested Scripture:

MATTHEW 9:9-13
MARK 2:13-17
LUKE 5:27-32

"LIKEWISE, NO ONE POURS NEW WINE INTO
OLD WINESKINS . . ."
(MK 2:22, NAB).

Why is it, Jesus, that as much as signs of change are all around me—nature, for instance, is one of your greatest teachers—I still find it hard to accept what time and life bring to me? It seems the rules are always changing. On one hand, I know that time is a gift, the healer of wounds, the place of possibility. On the other, it stands before me as mystery—the home of the unknown. I go to open the door of tomorrow, wrestling with these options. The crossing-over to newness becomes, itself, a cross that digs into my shoulder and burdens me instead. I wish I had the grace-fullness of the butterfly, allowing the wind to catch my wings and carry me forward and beyond.

Jesus: There is no mathematical equation for life, but the cross of yesterday can become the anchor of faith for all your tomorrows.

Suggested Scripture:

MATTHEW 9:14-17
MARK 2:18-22
LUKE 5:33-39

THE PHARISEES SAID TO [JESUS], "LOOK, WHY ARE THEY DOING WHAT IS NOT LAWFUL ON THE SABBATH?" (MK 2:24).

Jesus, when will we ever learn to mind our own business? Good intentions are subtle masks for the judgments we pass on one another. Sadly, even in the name of God, we hold some expectations that are really strong demands.

How many times do I expect others to live up to my ideals? Not that there is anything wrong, necessarily, with the goals I pursue; but those goals are mine—not another's. We are all on the same journey, but each time I expect someone to travel *my* path, I know that I become a burden instead of a companion.

I know, Jesus, I know—my way is *my* way; forgive me when I question any other. Forgive me when I judge what is in another person's heart. The harshness I bring when I do this is far from what you desire for me.

Jesus: Self-righteousness is like a heavy coat in the summer. It makes you and everyone else uncomfortable. Self-*rightness* rests so lightly that no one is aware when it is worn.

Suggested Scripture:

MATTHEW 12:1-8
MARK 2:23-28
LUKE 6:1-5

**[JESUS] LOOKED AROUND AT THEM WITH ANGER; HE WAS
GRIEVED AT THEIR HARDNESS OF HEART . . .
(MK 3:5).**

Missed opportunities! Is it fear that closes minds against you, Jesus? Do we fear the surprise of you? Is my mind so set in the ways I want you in my life that you are deeply grieved with me at times? Have I forbidden you to enter the temple of my heart because the time was not of my choosing? How presumptuous of me to think there is a right or wrong time for you!

Like the Pharisees, it was my loss, wasn't it, Jesus? Missed opportunities for healing, missed opportunities to celebrate your presence in my life. Do not grow impatient with me, Jesus. Do not let any shriveling of my mind or heart keep you from entering the sanctuary of my soul on any day.

Jesus: I surprise you when you make plans for me!

Suggested Scripture:

MATTHEW 12:9-14
MARK 3:1-6
LUKE 6:6-11

[JESUS] HAD CURED MANY AND, AS A RESULT, THOSE WHO HAD DISEASES WERE PRESSING UPON HIM TO TOUCH HIM (MK 3:10, NAB).

I don't know how you did it, Jesus. You never said, "No." You made space for yourself, but only so that you could offer more. Didn't you ever get tired of being pushed and pulled and touched and pleaded with? I have. No matter how much I do, there always seems to be one more person or one more thing that needs my attention. I just can't keep up with it sometimes.

Needs were endless for you, but you never complained. There's no place in the gospels that says you moaned and groaned. The only need you had was time for prayer. Time apart with your Father-God was refreshment enough. From there, you made yourself available— you became home, haven, and hope for everyone. It seems you needed so little to give so much.

Jesus: Perhaps if you put *me* on, you would not feel so put upon.

Suggested Scripture:

MATTHEW 12:15-21
MARK 3:7-12

SO HE APPOINTED THE TWELVE: SIMON (TO WHOM HE
GAVE THE NAME PETER) . . . AND JUDAS ISCARIOT,
WHO BETRAYED HIM
(MK 3:16-19).

Sometimes I wonder about you, Jesus. Your choice of disciples started with Peter, the impetuous know-it-all, and you went down the line to Judas, who would kiss you in betrayal. Why? You could see into people's hearts; you had to have some inkling about all of this! But that's just like you, Jesus, so full of hope for us. Maybe that's why I am counted among your followers—you want to give me a chance. Today, you invite me to move from my high-horse of knowing to clouds of unknowing, from the guilt of betrayal to the innocence of a child, from despair of myself to hope in you.

Yes, that is just like you, Jesus. I'm glad you didn't think twice about me. Thank you for a wisdom that is not of this world.

Jesus: Second chances are better than second thoughts.
Second chances put flesh on the hope of tomorrow.

Suggested Scripture:

MATTHEW 10:1-4
MARK 3:13-19
LUKE 6:12-16

WHEN HIS FAMILY HEARD . . . THEY WENT OUT TO RESTRAIN HIM FOR PEOPLE WERE SAYING, "[JESUS] HAS GONE OUT OF HIS MIND"
(MK 3:21).

Your family was trying to protect you, Jesus. No one wants to hear anything hurtful about a loved one. How difficult it must have been for them, knowing and loving you as they did. Even when they worried that you would wear yourself out, they knew that nothing would keep you from continuing your ways.

I think you wanted to protect them too; but how could you dampen the fire of zeal that consumed you? How could you quiet the voice of your actions and words—a voice meant to raise questions and challenge long-held beliefs? You couldn't . . . you wouldn't.

Jesus, how can I learn to let others live as they believe, without trying to rescue them from the hurt and misunderstanding that may follow? How can I better respect the choices of those I love and not impose my judgment, or even the fruit of my experience? I, too, care and mean well.

Jesus: Would it be better to save them from the lessons you learned, or allow them to become the teacher and guide of their own lives?

Suggested Scripture:

MARK 3:20-21

19

IF A KINGDOM IS DIVIDED AGAINST ITSELF, THAT KINGDOM CANNOT STAND
(MK 3:24).

Today I pray for peace, Jesus. In those places within me, where tension pulls at my heart, I ask for the reign of your healing instead. I know that I am a temple of God—the home of the holy. I do not wish to wage war against the sacred, but selfishness and greed climb the walls of my good intentions, steal into my spirit like a thief, and rob me of wholeness and peace.

If today I am to be held captive by anything or anyone, let it be you. Let it be the confrontation of desire with action. Let the walls I build be strongholds of wholeness, and sincerity be the only arms I bear, that loyalty may live where division once dwelled.

Jesus: Division is mended when threads of peace catch the weave of your life.

Suggested Scripture:

MATTHEW 12:22-32
MARK 3:22-30
LUKE 11:14-23

AND [JESUS] REPLIED, "WHO ARE MY MOTHER AND MY
BROTHERS? . . . HERE ARE MY MOTHER AND MY BROTH-
ERS! WHOEVER DOES THE WILL OF GOD IS MY BROTHER
AND SISTER AND MOTHER"

(MK 3:33-35).

At first I am taken back, Jesus, that nameless faces
have kinship with you equal to your mother. Had you
given no thought to her feelings? We do. We place her on
a pedestal, clothe her in blue and white, honor her with
songs, and crown her with flowers. Is our respect for her
greater than yours? No, that could never be. Your invitation to family bonds is sealed with the will of God. It is
from there that you raise her to greatness.

Jesus, I do not think that I could rise to such
heights—be as open to the Spirit, as understanding of
your challenges, as faithful and long-suffering as your
mother. How can I become one of the family when I feel
so much like an outsider?

Jesus: When you bear me in the womb of your faith,
God's will is born on the earth. This is the tie that
binds us.

Suggested Scripture:

MATTHEW 12:46-50
MARK 3:31-35
LUKE 8:19-21

AND [JESUS] SAID TO THEM, "DO YOU NOT UNDERSTAND THIS PARABLE? . . . THE SOWER SOWS THE WORD" (MK 4:13-14).

Everyone likes a good story, Jesus, especially one with a happy ending. Yours didn't start off so well today. That farmer was rather careless, the way he sowed his field; rather indiscriminate, wasting seed on worthless ground. Lucky for him the harvest was rich! You'd think he would have planned more wisely. Then you tell us that this seed is the word of God. Are you sure? Of course you are. How extravagant God is!

Jesus: If my Father did not cast me so freely upon this earth, I could never have become bread for so many.

Suggested Scripture:

MATTHEW 13:1-23
MARK 4:1-20
LUKE 8:4-15

[JESUS] SAID TO THEM, "IS A LAMP BROUGHT IN TO BE PUT
UNDER THE BUSHEL BASKET, OR UNDER THE BED, AND NOT
ON THE LAMPSTAND?"
(MK 4:21).

I know, Jesus, that I am that lamp. You hold me before
the face of the earth and say, "Let there be light!" But the
brightness that you wish me to shed becomes a burden at
times; there is so much darkness in our world. You tell me,
today, not to measure what I give because God will give
to me beyond all measure. Are you sure that I will not
burn out? How can my light reach the four corners of the
earth where my brothers and sisters dwell? I need some
assurance that my efforts will not be in vain, that the
flame of my life will not be quenched by the flood of so
many needs.

Jesus: True, you are the lamp, but I am the constant
source of your light.

Suggested Scripture:

MARK 4:21-25
LUKE 8:16-18

... "THE KINGDOM OF GOD IS AS IF SOMEONE WOULD SCATTER SEED ON THE GROUND, AND WOULD SLEEP AND RISE NIGHT AND DAY, AND THE SEED WOULD SPROUT AND GROW, HE DOES NOT KNOW HOW"

(MK 4:26-27).

This farmer is a believer, Jesus. He goes about his daily tasks with confidence—trusting he has prepared the soil well enough, trusting the rains to water the fields, trusting the seed itself to be about its nature. Is God a believer, too, Jesus—a believer in me? Perhaps. Planting me on this earth, God trusts that all will go well—all will work to good. To assure this work, I know I was given you, Jesus, should I, unlike the seed, forget my true nature and never unearth my capabilities.

If my farmer-God has such faith in me, help me, Jesus, to believe as much in myself. Let me trust the seed of my life, believing that in you my grounding was well prepared; that within this seed a kernel of hope is always ready to burst into new life.

Jesus: The farmer can sleep so peacefully because his dreams are the meeting place of God's desires.

Suggested Scripture:

MATTHEW 13:31-32
MARK 4:26-34
LUKE 13:18-19

... "LET US GO ACROSS TO THE OTHER SIDE." AND LEAVING THE CROWD BEHIND, THEY TOOK [JESUS] WITH THEM IN THE BOAT ...
(MK 4:35-36).

I doubt the disciples knew what they were getting into, Jesus, when you suggested the farther shore. Having made the trip many times, they set out on familiar waters quite unsuspecting of surprises. Suddenly, a storm—waves cresting over the boat until all feared drowning. All but you—you were asleep. What knocked and buffeted the disciples into fear rocked you into blessed sleep.

Sometimes I set out for farther shores, expecting nothing unusual, and suddenly my life is blown off course. It is hard for me to believe that I will reach the other side when waves of the unexpected nearly drown my hopes and dreams. How can you sleep at times like these?

Jesus: Awake or asleep does not matter. Remember—I, too, am in the boat.

Suggested Scripture:

MATTHEW 8:23-27
MARK 4:35-41
LUKE 8:22-25

A Cup of Grace:

WHEN [JESUS] GOT OUT OF THE BOAT, AT ONCE A MAN . . .
WHO HAD AN UNCLEAN SPIRIT MET HIM. THE MAN HAD
BEEN DWELLING AMONG THE TOMBS, AND NO ONE COULD
RESTRAIN HIM ANY LONGER . . .

(MK 5:2-3, NAB).

No one proved strong enough except you, Jesus. How tortured that man must have been, unable to have control over his very self; invaded by forces beyond his own comprehension and strength. How he must have longed, in his heart of hearts, to be free of the pain he caused himself and others. How lonely he must have felt, lost in a land that would always separate him from society, an alien to them and to himself.

You released him from that pain, Jesus. You did not resort to handcuffs and chains to calm him, but only your word—the word of God. Jesus, when I feel invaded by fear beyond my comprehension and anxiety beyond my control; when my heart longs for freedom or weeps with loneliness; when I am a foreigner in the land of my own being, then speak your word to me. Be strong enough to tame my fear and anxiety; unchain me from my desolation; free me from my isolation. No one is strong enough except you, Jesus. No one, except you.

Jesus: I will always hear your cries. I am held captive by
          the needs of your heart.

Suggested Scripture:

MATTHEW 8:28–9:1
MARK 5:1-20
LUKE 8:26-39

JESUS, AWARE AT ONCE THAT POWER HAD GONE OUT
FROM HIM, TURNED AROUND IN THE CROWD AND ASKED,
"WHO HAS TOUCHED MY CLOTHES?"
(MK 5:30, NAB).

Often I think I take you for granted, Jesus. I focus on the mystery of your healing and forget that what you freely gave to others exacted a price from you. As the flow of holy energy left you to stem the tide of this woman's blood, was your strength ebbed as well? When you awakened Jairus's daughter, did you feel the heaviness of her sleep? Each time you healed the blind, did your eyes know a moment of darkness? If so, why do you continue to give, to heal, to restore us to life? Why do you continue to allow me to come to you, to take from you, to find you in my brokenness? Why, Jesus?

Jesus: For me, nothing is ever lost. It is just the cost of loving.

Suggested Scripture:

MATTHEW 9:18-26
MARK 5:21-43
LUKE 8:40-56

... "PROPHETS ARE NOT WITHOUT HONOR, EXCEPT IN
THEIR HOMETOWN, AND AMONG THEIR OWN KIN, AND IN
THEIR OWN HOUSE"
(MK 6:4).

I am saddened for you today, Jesus. I guess the saying is true—"you can't go home again." This was your hometown, yet the hands of the carpenter's son, once praised for their craft, became the object of cynicism that day. I should think that familiarity would nurture faith, not fear. Your neighbors seemed to be threatened by your success instead of grateful for your gifts.

There are times when I have difficulty listening to the people I know so well. Instead of believing and trusting family or friends, I sometimes go elsewhere to seek truth, knowledge, even talent. Why do I act this way? What need do I try to fill? Do I label the lives of others to limit their success? Is that what is necessary to find a comfort zone in life?

Jesus: If cynicism is your only comfort, then the doors of your home will be closed even to you.

Suggested Scripture:

MATTHEW 13:54-58
MARK 6:1-6
LUKE 4:16-30

[JESUS] INSTRUCTED THEM TO TAKE NOTHING FOR THE
JOURNEY BUT A WALKING STICK—NO FOOD, NO SACK, NO
MONEY IN THEIR BELTS
(MK 6:8, NAB).

Jesus, a walking stick? Really, I don't know how you kept those disciples with you! And why were you so sure they would get the job done—you didn't even allow them the necessities? It's one thing for you to have few needs, but why ask your friends to deprive themselves? Weren't you being a bit unreasonable? Were you not concerned for their safety and well-being?

In light of your instruction today, Jesus, I live a rather indulgent and cluttered life. I do not lack for anything. In fact, in some cases, I have more than I need. Can I still be one of your disciples? A walking stick alone just doesn't make it in today's world. Isn't this all a bit naive?

Jesus: No. You see, I gave you one another.

Suggested Scripture:

MATTHEW 10:5-15
MARK 6:7-13
LUKE 9:1-6

BUT WHEN HEROD LEARNED OF [THE HEALING POWER OF
JESUS], HE SAID, "JOHN, WHOM I BEHEADED,
HAS BEEN RAISED"
(MK 6:16).

Herod sounds afraid, Jesus. Did he think you came to taunt him with the memory of John? To haunt him with the memory of actions regretted too late? Herod took on a heavy burden when he allowed pride to be a guest at his table. It seems guilt became the nightmare of his soul. I imagine he was never quite the same after that. Perhaps he lost even his appetite for celebration.

Sometimes I feel like Herod, Jesus. There are things I, too, regret—actions too quickly taken, even deeds committed, fully knowing their consequences. I, too, have abused the power to choose. It is then that the ghost of guilt haunts my soul as well.

Jesus: Let that guilt goad you into change. The bitterness of regret will sweeten with this wisdom.

Suggested Scripture:

MATTHEW 14:1-12
MARK 6:14-29
LUKE 9:7-9

[JESUS] SAID TO THEM, "COME AWAY TO A DESERTED
PLACE ALL BY YOURSELVES AND REST A WHILE."
FOR MANY WERE COMING AND GOING,
AND THEY HAD NO LEISURE EVEN TO EAT
(MK 6:31).

Jesus, you saw the need to get away. It was a sensible decision, given that your apostles hadn't had a moment's peace even to eat. You knew the need for balance. You knew the kingdom of God would come about by good judgment as well as by good works.

I tend to be an overachiever, finding it hard to know when to stop. I suppose that somewhere along the line I learned that nothing is ever enough, so I do more and more and more. I could use a little of your common sense, Jesus.

Jesus: At times, common sense is compassion turned inward.

Suggested Scripture:

MATTHEW 14:13-21
MARK 6:30-34
LUKE 9:10-17
JOHN 6:1-14

AND WHEREVER [JESUS] WENT . . . THEY LAID THE SICK IN
THE MARKETPLACES, AND BEGGED HIM THAT THEY MIGHT
TOUCH EVEN THE FRINGE OF HIS CLOAK; AND ALL WHO
TOUCHED IT WERE HEALED
(MK 6:56).

All who touch you get well, Jesus. What was it like
to know your whole being was so committed to healing,
giving, forgiving—that for someone to touch even your
clothing would be an experience of spontaneous grace?
How absolutely free you were! How absolutely free!

There must be a key to your freedom; a key that I can
turn to open the lock to my heart—the lock that keeps
me from giving so fully, so easily. The free gift of your life
remains my deepest desire . . . to give as freely as you.

Jesus: This key you desire is not hidden. If you were to
touch me, you, too, would find it in the folds of
my cloak.

Suggested Scripture:

MATTHEW 14:34-36
MARK 6:53-56

**SO THE PHARISEES AND THE SCRIBES ASKED [JESUS],
"WHY DO YOUR DISCIPLES NOT LIVE ACCORDING TO THE
TRADITION OF THE ELDERS . . . ?"
(MK 7:5).**

How easy it is to cling to the past, Jesus. As much as I try, at times I fall into that pattern as well. I believe in the weave of yesterday with today, but sometimes yesterday is safer; the tried and true got me where I am today.

There I go again! To be honest, Jesus, this path of the past doesn't always bring me to tomorrow. I wish I knew a better way of weaving; maybe I'd be more inclined to "drop a stitch" and less compelled to retrieve it.

Jesus: It is each day's weaving that gives richness to yesterday's threads.

Suggested Scripture:

MATTHEW 15:1-9
MARK 7:1-13

[JESUS] SUMMONED THE CROWD AGAIN AND SAID TO
THEM, "HEAR ME, ALL OF YOU, AND UNDERSTAND.
NOTHING THAT ENTERS ONE FROM OUTSIDE CAN DEFILE
THAT PERSON; BUT THE THINGS THAT COME OUT FROM
WITHIN ARE WHAT DEFILE"
(MK 7:14-15, NAB).

Jesus, these are welcoming words to the child within us. We were born of God, you remind us; our truth makes us holy and whole. Why do we doubt ourselves when we were conceived in the heart of God? No words, actions, or accidents can change that!

You meant to set me free by this truth today, Jesus. Help me not to believe what I may have heard or received in the past—the words and actions of discouragement that turned me to fear even myself. Remind me that I am greater and grander than any of my memories. Help me to understand that I first rested in the womb of a parenting God, nurtured first and foremost by grace. Let this message of hope replay itself over and over again in my heart, that I might be brave.

Jesus: I will make it your deepest memory, but you must recall it each day.

Suggested Scripture:

MATTHEW 15:10-20
MARK 7:14-23

[JESUS] SAID TO HER, "LET THE CHILDREN BE FED FIRST,
FOR IT IS NOT FAIR TO TAKE THE CHILDREN'S FOOD AND
THROW IT TO THE DOGS." BUT SHE ANSWERED HIM, "SIR,
EVEN THE DOGS UNDER THE TABLE
EAT THE CHILDREN'S CRUMBS"
(MK 7:27-28).

I doubt that you could ever withhold yourself from us, Jesus—especially if we came carrying the faith of this woman. The dialogue between the two of you isn't meant to be a power struggle for the sake of Israel but the empowerment of all who would believe.

The banquet of salvation has no reserved seating. And even crumbs from this table hold the fullness of healing and life. This Gentile woman gives me the courage to approach this table despite any sin or failing that I fear might separate me from you. She gives me a new perspective on the "little things" of life. She makes me want to gather up the fragments and find, there, a feast.

Jesus: If you learn how to feast on broken bread, you will become whole.

Suggested Scripture:

MATTHEW 15:21-28
MARK 7:24-30

[JESUS] . . . PUT HIS FINGERS INTO [THE MAN'S] EARS,
AND HE SPAT AND TOUCHED HIS TONGUE. THEN LOOKING
UP TO HEAVEN, [JESUS] SIGHED AND SAID TO HIM,
"EPHPHATHA," THAT IS, "BE OPENED"
(MK 7:33-34).

The power of touch, Jesus. We so underestimate that simple, yet profound communication of human presence. When you healed the man in today's story, you went directly to the place of his need. "Yes," you tell us, "Yes, I know exactly the place of your anguish, your anxiety, your pain. And I share wholeness with you through the healing spirit of my own body."

You show me that nothing is profane for you. The most basic, even visceral realities are instruments of your healing grace. Give me, then, the wisdom to know the true needs of those I may meet today; the courage to spend my very self in free grace; and the vision to see the holy in all things.

Jesus: Do not hesitate to go to places of pain. That, itself, can be the healing . . . for you will meet me there.

Suggested Scripture:

MATTHEW 15:29-31
MARK 7:31-37

[JESUS'] DISCIPLES ANSWERED HIM, "WHERE CAN ANYONE
GET ENOUGH BREAD TO SATISFY THEM HERE IN THIS
DESERTED PLACE?"
(MK 8:4, NAB).

Jesus, how fully aware you are of the needs of your people. How quickly compassion moved you to action. Reality stood before you, wearing the face of your disciples carrying seven loaves of bread and a few small fish. Yet the impossible became possible—love always finds a way.

Today you encourage me to compassion and possibilities. Reality stands before me as well. Yet in times of need, Jesus, if I remain standing there, I will be in the way—blocking the way. You challenge me to stand alongside the realities of my day as you did. Then as companions, we will walk toward the poor together. But, Jesus, I still have so little. . . .

Jesus: The impossible becomes possible, if you start with what you have, however small.

Suggested Scripture:

MATTHEW 15:32-39
MARK 8:1-10

[JESUS] SIGHED FROM THE DEPTH OF HIS SPIRIT AND SAID,
"WHY DOES THIS GENERATION SEEK A SIGN? . . ."
(MK 8:12, NAB).

Today I think you would say to us, "What you see is what you get!" Yet this need for signs, Jesus, is not just a reality of long ago—I'm not much different from the Pharisees. Yes, I know that mystery is not meant to be a burden, but signs would make life's mysteries a bit easier to bear.

You know that about me, yet you challenge me to look beyond my need to see, that I may see in my need—that I may see you. Is my faith so weak because my vision is so narrow? How then might I focus on you? These earth-eyes of mine are often tempted to search the stars. How can this need to see starlight lead to you?

Jesus: Widen the path of your vision and epiphany will shine in the night.

Suggested Scripture:

MATTHEW 16:1-4
MARK 8:11-13

AND [JESUS] CAUTIONED THEM SAYING, "WATCH OUT—
BEWARE OF THE YEAST OF THE PHARISEES AND THE YEAST
OF HEROD." THEY SAID TO ONE ANOTHER, "IT IS BECAUSE
WE HAVE NO BREAD"
(MK 8:15-16).

Jesus, I am tempted to think that anyone as close to you as your disciples would understand your words. Yet I sometimes see only the surface, the more obvious, the easily grasped, missing the deeper issue. Nevertheless, it must have been frustrating for you, feeling the urgency to teach so much with so little time.

Today you challenge me, once again, to go deeper. You do not mean to pose riddles but to make me think and evaluate what I hear, or read, or encounter. The yeast of the Pharisees—the influence of their teaching—produces a loaf of bread that is weak in nutrients, a loaf that hasn't risen to its fullness. "Beware," you tell me, "beware of anything that does not enhance, nourish, and fulfill your life."

Jesus, how can I become more aware, more discerning of the bread I choose to break?

Jesus: When someone offers you bread, ask to see the field of wheat from which it came.

Suggested Scripture:

MATTHEW 16:5-12
MARK 8:14-21

[JESUS AND HIS DISCIPLES] CAME TO BETHSAIDA. SOME
PEOPLE BROUGHT A BLIND MAN TO [JESUS] AND BEGGED
HIM TO TOUCH HIM
(MK 8:22).

People begged you to touch them, Jesus. They weren't shy, but perhaps this blind man was and needed his friends to do the asking. For me, the hardest time to ask for help is when I need it most; I'm no longer in control then. I tell myself that I don't want to burden others but, more honestly, I don't want to admit that I need their help.

But that's exactly what you want me to do—ASK. Touching me with healing is what you want to do, what you are most anxious to do. So Jesus, thank you for my friends, for people who know me better than I know myself at times, for people who willingly, gladly take me in prayer to you when I do not go as readily. Touch them too.

Jesus: Yes, for I mean you to be support for one another—not as crutches but as the columns of a temple.

Suggested Scripture:

MARK 8:22-26

... ON THE WAY [JESUS] ASKED HIS DISCIPLES, "WHO DO PEOPLE SAY THAT I AM?" AND THEY ANSWERED HIM, "JOHN THE BAPTIST; AND OTHERS, ELIJAH; AND STILL OTHERS, ONE OF THE PROPHETS." HE ASKED THEM, "BUT WHO DO YOU SAY THAT I AM?"
(MK 8:27-29).

You posed the same question twice, Jesus—first, in general; second, quite personally. This is the way I come to know you, isn't it? First, I hear others speak of you—my parents and grandparents, a teacher, a friend. It is from their faith and experience of God that you extend to me your invitation to friendship and lifelong companionship.

Then comes the time when Jesus of the Christmas crib becomes Jesus of the cross. You have much to share with me and others along this road, so do not let me hesitate to follow you. I have long lost my illusions, Jesus; remind me that now you illumine my way. Take away my fears and free me for new life.

Jesus: Just believe that any detours you encounter can still become the path to me.

Suggested Scripture:

MATTHEW 16:13-20
MARK 8:27-33
LUKE 9:18-20

A Cup of Grace:

"FOR THOSE WHO WANT TO SAVE THEIR LIFE WILL LOSE IT, AND THOSE WHO LOSE THEIR LIFE FOR MY SAKE, AND FOR THE SAKE OF THE GOSPEL, WILL SAVE IT"
(MK 8:35).

Letting go of anything I love is not easy, Jesus, but losing my life when my most basic instinct is to preserve it? These are very hard words you speak to me today, very hard. I have long understood that whatever you ask me is no more or no less than what you have asked of yourself, but still it is not an easy road to walk. I respect this martyr-life but need you to keep me from becoming a victim. Justice and truth will put *me* on the line. Keep me willing to lay down my life along this path. Teach me how to live without compromise, yet with love. Justice and truth require courage from me, and gentleness as well.

I count on you to be there, Jesus. And in the end, when I breathe my last, draw me in with your breath of new life.

Jesus: Each time you climb the wood of the cross, you walk the path to resurrection.

Suggested Scripture:

MATTHEW 16:21-28
MARK 8:31-9:1
LUKE 9:21-27

THEN PETER SAID TO JESUS, "RABBI, IT IS GOOD FOR US
TO BE HERE; LET US MAKE THREE DWELLINGS, ONE FOR
YOU, ONE FOR MOSES, AND ONE FOR ELIJAH"
(MK 9:5).

Peace is like that; I want to stay with it as long as I can—build peace a house to protect it, and myself, from the storms of life. It sounds like a good idea, Jesus, but I know that nothing lasts forever, and the shelters of all my efforts would only become prisons for all my hopes.

Yes, Jesus, it is good for me to be here, but you tell me that it is just as good, and necessary, to move on. "Let us leave this place," you said. I suppose only then can I anticipate a return. Help me then, Jesus. Help me to climb down from my mountains of satisfaction, to walk the plains of the ordinary for a while. Help me down, but let me down easy; the climb looks steep and it's awfully hard to leave this place of peace.

Jesus: Peace is not a mountain to climb. Peace lives in the climber.

Suggested Scripture:

MATTHEW 17:1-13
MARK 9:2-13
LUKE 9:28-36

JESUS SAID TO HIM, ". . . ALL THINGS CAN BE DONE FOR
THE ONE WHO BELIEVES"
(MK 9:23).

Really, Jesus—all things? That's almost too good to be true! You hold out hope to me today, and ask for faith in return. I find myself echoing the response of that man, "I believe; help my unbelief."

I want to believe, Jesus, not just for selfish reasons, not just because all my needs would be met by such faith, but because of you—just you. I want to wrap my faith and trust around your love for me, and give them back to you as gifts. I feel so poor, many days, in what I have to offer you by word and action; I want so much to give you this—this least, yet most basic gift of myself. I believe in you, Jesus; help my unbelief.

Jesus: Your desire is faith enough; for in desire, faith is made complete.

Suggested Scripture:

MATTHEW 17:14-21
MARK 9:14-29
LUKE 9:37-43

... "WHOEVER WANTS TO BE FIRST MUST BE LAST OF ALL
AND SERVANT OF ALL. . . . WHOEVER WELCOMES ONE
SUCH CHILD IN MY NAME WELCOMES ME . . ."
(MK 9:35-37).

Life can be so competitive, Jesus. Sometimes over-and-against seems the only way to scratch out an existence, keep a job, feed a family. Everything around me encourages a top-of-the-line, me-first attitude. But today you offer a little child to lead me in the way. Here greatness is not measured by first against last, but by meekness of a gentle heart.

Help me, then, to discover in myself this child who, perhaps, has lost the way. Let me find my place in this world without the necessity of fighting to be first in line. May I be the one to stand ready at the door, welcoming that child . . . sitting down with servant-hospitality.

Jesus: Simplicity is a lasting gift of welcome.

Suggested Scripture:

MATTHEW 17:22, 18:1-5
MARK 9:30-37
LUKE 9:43-48

A Cup of Grace:

Jesus, your disciples were very protective of you. Unfortunately they failed to see as good the works performed by another, that person who was not one of them. Am I like that, Jesus? Do I miss the accomplishments of others because they were not accomplished by me, my way? I know my way is not the only way, and that sometimes my vision is narrow; my planning, rigid; my expectations, too few. Yet I do this again and again.

Today, you remind me that many roads lead to you; that many, together for the good, can bring good about in many ways. Jesus, open my eyes, make flexible my planning, multiply my expectations so that my judgment may not lessen another's good but, happily, affirm it.

Jesus: Good judgment is the fruit of an open heart—a heart grateful for all that is great.

Suggested Scripture:

MATTHEW 10:40-42
MARK 9:38-40
LUKE 9:49-50

"IF YOUR HAND CAUSES YOU TO SIN, CUT IT OFF. IT IS BETTER FOR YOU TO ENTER INTO LIFE MAIMED THAN WITH TWO HANDS TO GO INTO GEHENNA . . ."
(MK 9:43, NAB).

These are hard sayings of yours, Jesus. I can get so caught up, at times, with physical perfection that repulsion could easily keep me from the deeper meaning of your words today. I protest that I need both eyes, both hands, both feet—after all, how would I be able to do your work effectively without them?

Maybe I protest too much. Maybe I should ask myself just how well I've used my eyes to see your presence, my hands to do your work, my feet to follow you in the ways of justice, charity, and peace. Perhaps I need to take some drastic measures with my heart instead—seek honesty and there find my wholeness.

Jesus: It is the heart that sees, touches, and moves you. The body simply follows the way of your heart.

Suggested Scripture:

MATHEW 18:6-9
MARK 9:41-50
LUKE 17:1-2

[THE PHARISEES] SAID, "MOSES ALLOWED A MAN TO WRITE A CERTIFICATE OF DISMISSAL AND TO DIVORCE [HIS WIFE]." BUT JESUS SAID TO THEM, "BECAUSE OF YOUR HARDNESS OF HEART HE WROTE THIS COMMANDMENT FOR YOU"
(MK 10:4-5).

God has made many concessions to my weaknesses, Jesus. Nothing I do can keep me from forgiveness and love. Why does God do this? Why meet me on the road of temptation and sin, again and again, and hold healing out before me? And why did you say "yes" to become the heart of this great plan of abundant love?

It is so difficult for me to understand such generosity! I know I'm not off the hook, though. I know I have a part in this homecoming. I know that you call me to rise to the occasion of your grace. I know that first I, alone, must put my foot on the path and follow you—but still, your trust in me is so astounding!

Jesus: It is my hope that your "surprise" today will become a holy expectation one day.

Suggested Scripture:

MATTHEW 19:1-9
MARK 10:1-12

PEOPLE WERE BRINGING LITTLE CHILDREN TO [JESUS]. . . .
AND HE TOOK THEM UP IN HIS ARMS, LAID HIS HANDS ON
THEM, AND BLESSED THEM
(MK 10:13-16).

Jesus, leave it to you to put things into perspective. The disciples probably feared that children would be a bother or distraction to you; after all, the kingdom of God was serious business and someone had to handle the crowd. But you didn't turn away children. You touched, embraced, and blessed them instead. So while your disciples were trying to save time, you were willing to squander it, or so it seems.

Teach me, today, to take time out from what I view as the serious business of my life, not to waste it but to balance my life with time—for the child within me still needs your blessing and embrace.

Jesus: At times your cares are best served by the care-lessness of a child.

Suggested Scripture:

MATTHEW 19:13-15
MARK 10:13-16
LUKE 18:15-17

A Cup of Grace:

> **. . . A MAN RAN UP AND KNELT BEFORE [JESUS], AND ASKED HIM, "GOOD TEACHER, WHAT MUST I DO TO INHERIT ETERNAL LIFE?"**
> **(MK 10:17).**

Yes, Jesus, how will I be sure I am going to heaven? Give me some rule of thumb that I can measure myself by. I keep the commandments . . . most times; yet I wonder if I, too, am lacking something. I don't mean to be a worrier, but I need to be sure I am making the grade in grace. I want to cover all the bases so that, when this life is over, I won't have played a losing game.

You know the human heart so well, and I can often fool myself. Lead me into the heart of your knowing.

Jesus: Remember as you run to win the prize, I give grace freely. You do not occasion the gift.

Suggested Scripture:

MATTHEW 19:16-26
MARK 10:17-27
LUKE 18:18-27

JESUS SAID, "TRULY I TELL YOU, THERE IS NO ONE WHO
HAS LEFT HOUSE OR BROTHERS OR SISTERS OR MOTHER OR
FATHER OR CHILDREN OR FIELDS, FOR MY SAKE AND FOR
THE SAKE OF THE GOOD NEWS, WHO WILL NOT RECEIVE A
HUNDREDFOLD NOW IN THIS AGE . . ."
(MK 10:29-30).

Peter's need to know that all was not in vain is the opportunity for me to hear of God's providential love once again. But why do I find it so hard to remember? Often I can count my crosses quicker than my blessings. Are the blessings not as obvious? Or is my perception impaired by some religious ethic that says, "If it hurts, it's holy"?

Jesus, you came to us to set things straight, to set us straight. As your Father-God knew your needs, God knows mine as well. Joy is here now, too, not in some far off time that only suffering will reveal. Open my eyes to see the hundredfold you hold out to me this day.

Jesus: God does not judge with divine wrath but with divine love.

Suggested Scripture:

MATTHEW 19:27-30
MARK 10:28-31
LUKE 18:28-30

A Cup of Grace:

JAMES AND JOHN . . . SAID TO [JESUS], "TEACHER, WE
WANT YOU TO DO FOR US WHATEVER WE ASK OF YOU. . . .
GRANT US TO SIT, ONE AT YOUR RIGHT HAND AND ONE AT
YOUR LEFT, IN YOUR GLORY"
(MK 10:35-37).

Jesus, I must admit that my prayer begins that way at times. I begin asking for what I want and then proceed to tell you how it must come about. My words leave no room for the mystery of you. Maybe that is what I try to avoid—the mystery—the mystery of you and the mystery of life in you.

James and John raced right to the prize of glory. They saw only their goal, not the road that would lead them there. Sometimes I find the road a little frightening, Jesus, and I realize that my prayer left no room for the journey it would entail. Help me then to pray my needs but with a greater willingness to accept the cup or baptism that your answer may bring.

Jesus: You must empty your plans from the cup of your prayer, if I am to fill it.

Suggested Scripture:

MATTHEW 20:17-28
MARK 10:32-45
LUKE 8:32-34

. . . THE BLIND MAN SAID TO [JESUS], "MY TEACHER, LET ME SEE AGAIN" (MK 10:51).

Jesus, some days . . . sometimes I, too, am blind. What once was so clear to me becomes hazy, and I panic. Life moves around me as shadows cast by my fears. I know it's a matter of control; I prefer the driver's seat, but that's not very wise, for often I do not even know the way. Yet, a passenger's life is not for me, Jesus, so I sit in the house of my determination and let the storm clouds of fear sweep over me. It's then that I pave a road to nowhere with my stubbornness.

Jesus, let me see again. But if this blindness is leading me to you somehow, teach me how to go along for the ride.

Jesus: Let me take the wheel, and you will no longer be driven by fear.

Suggested Scripture:

MATTHEW 20:29-34
MARK 10:46-52
LUKE 18:35-43

... ON ENTERING THE TEMPLE AREA [JESUS] BEGAN TO
DRIVE OUT THOSE SELLING AND BUYING THERE. ... THEN
HE TAUGHT THEM SAYING, "IS IT NOT WRITTEN: 'MY
HOUSE SHALL BE CALLED A HOUSE OF PRAYER FOR ALL
PEOPLES'? BUT YOU HAVE MADE IT A DEN OF THIEVES"
(MK 11:15-17, NAB).

Jesus, if you were to enter my human temple—the dwelling place of God within me—would you find a house of prayer there? Would you find a heart set on God alone? I know that in some places, yes, but not everywhere. There are corners in which I ply the trade of selfishness, judgment, envy, and pride. Yes, I know you would find these places, Jesus, however hidden they may be.

But you have already been there, haven't you? Today, every day, you invite me to show those "traders" the way out. Help me to clear away this clutter and to bring light—you, Jesus—into those corners of my life.

Jesus: I seek the corners of your heart, not to expose weakness, but to impose my hands of healing.

Suggested Scripture:

MATTHEW 21:12-22
MARK 11:11-26
LUKE 19:45-48
JOHN 2:13-22

. . . As [Jesus] was walking in the temple, the chief priests, the scribes, and the elders came to him and said, "By what authority are you doing these things?" (Mk 11:27-28).

It seems wherever you go, Jesus, the opportunity for questions and debate is fast on your heels. Ironically, the tension grows with each miracle, word, or action of yours. I wonder if my faith would cause such an uproar? Do my actions or words generate an energy of conviction that would cause others even to notice my belief?

Jesus, you could see into their hearts. You know my heart as well; perhaps that is where challenge and debate must first begin for me. I do not think I hold the lamp of your authority high enough, at times, to illumine the reasons for all that I do. Forgive my questioning of you, for I hesitate to question myself as well. The dilemma of these religious people is also my undoing.

Jesus: Questions need not be the cords that bind you, but the core of truth that sets you free.

Suggested Scripture:

Matthew 21:23-27
Mark 11:27-33
Luke 20:1-8

> "HAVE YOU NOT READ THIS SCRIPTURE: 'THE STONE THAT
> THE BUILDERS REJECTED HAS BECOME THE
> CORNERSTONE; THIS WAS THE LORD'S DOING, AND IT IS
> AMAZING IN OUR EYES'?"
> (MK 12:10-11).

It is hard to believe that people could have rejected you, Jesus. All you wanted to do was widen the boundaries of faith. You never intended to destroy the foundation, yet your invitation to sit down at the drawing table, together, was far too threatening for some. The peace you offered wasn't the "piece" they were looking for. You just didn't fit into their conception of the kingdom.

I'd like to think that I wouldn't have been as suspicious or fearful, but I wonder, today, what edifice I build and protect with my life? Who invites me, Jesus, to climb those walls and see things from a different perspective? How guarded am I against views that might stretch the dimensions of my thinking?

Jesus: As you draw the blueprint of your life, allow for many ways of entry. The home of your heart is better served by hospitality than by the fear of hostility.

Suggested Scripture:

MATTHEW 21:33-46
MARK 12:1-12
LUKE 20:9-19

**. . . "GIVE TO THE EMPEROR THE THINGS
THAT ARE THE EMPEROR'S, AND TO GOD THE
THINGS THAT ARE GOD'S" . . .
(MK 12:17).**

Your words, Jesus, easily put the scale of life into balance. The formula is so simple; yet ironically, to attain it seems so complex. Or do I make it that way?

Sometimes I feel the divine and the human within me are at odds. Each day, I go off carrying responsibility on my shoulders and God in my heart, or so I think, but too often I come home stooped, burdened, and empty of heart. I'm a little off balance, it seems. What am I doing wrong?

Jesus: Perhaps there is no wrongdoing. Shift the weight a little to another day. Maybe your sense of responsibility far outweighs what the day requires.

Suggested Scripture:

MATTHEW 22:15-22
MARK 12:13-17
LUKE 20:20-26

JESUS SAID TO THEM, "IS NOT THIS THE REASON YOU ARE WRONG, THAT YOU KNOW NEITHER THE SCRIPTURES NOR THE POWER OF GOD?"
(MK 12:24).

Jesus, what started out as a trap for you became the opportunity for teaching, instead. Your words break through the dense fog of my own doubt and disbelief. You challenge me to end my frantic efforts of human rationalization so that the reality of God might stand free to simply be.

Hope in the resurrection will never be based on my efforts alone, for it was you who overcame death and offer new life. So why do I try? Why do I keep trying to figure out something so far beyond the limits of my human understanding? Perhaps the force of fear drives me into that dark night, compelling me to see what no eye has yet seen on this earth? Ah, maybe that's the point, Jesus—I presume that it is possible to see it here and now. Then, free me from the traps I set for eternal life. Free me, for it is I who am held fast.

Jesus: At times, the best answer—the only answer—is to stop asking the question.

Suggested Scripture:

MATTHEW 22:23-33
MARK 12:18-27
LUKE 20:27-40

> ". . . THE SECOND IS THIS, 'YOU SHALL LOVE YOUR
> NEIGHBOR AS YOURSELF' . . ."
> **(MK 12:31).**

I could almost say it is easier to love God with the fullness of my being—heart, soul, mind, and strength—than to live according to this second commandment. But that would be ivory-tower living, wouldn't it, Jesus? The gift of my love depends upon the presence of both—a truth I cannot escape, a reality beyond my deceit.

In many ways, I have known this and have done my fair share for the homeless, served in soup kitchens, given money to the poor. Today, though, your word strikes a more intimate chord in my heart. And I see that my neighbor has a face, an everyday face—the people with whom I live, work, meet, and speak to every day. Here there can be no grand gesture of anonymity. So, Jesus, help me to love the neighbors at my right hand and left with the same deep and honest love I would my God.

Jesus: When you turn toward your neighbor, it is toward your God.

Suggested Scripture:

MATTHEW 22:34-40
MARK 12:28-34
LUKE 10:25-28

A Cup of Grace:

What was true for David is true for me, Jesus, if I take the time to focus on the presence of God—but I must take the time. That's my problem; I can be so easily distracted by activity or thoughts, even in the name of charity. I deceive myself into believing that my best prayer, at times, is my work. Not that it can never be, but I too often excuse myself from the challenging work of prayer.

I keep running to the well of my being, filling bucket after bucket to quench the thirst of others. One day, I will exhaust that well, I know; it would be foolish to think otherwise. So slow me down, Jesus. Teach me how to slow my steps enough to notice you sitting beside my well. You know that is what I really want—you are what I really want.

Jesus: The Spirit inspires the work of your hands when you nurture the stirrings of your heart.

Suggested Scripture:

MATTHEW 22:41-46
MARK 12:35-37
LUKE 20:41-44

"Blessed are the peacemakers, for they will be called children of God" (Mt 5:9).

It's not a matter of refraining from war, is it, Jesus? After all, my chances of going to war are next to nothing. Today, I hear your words of blessed peace a bit closer to home because, at times, the battleground can be my very heart. My weapons are hurt feelings that I fashion, skillfully, into a sword to wield against the cause of a moment's pain.

Help me, Jesus. Help me to soften the sharpness of my desire to pay back an eye for an eye. Warm the coldness of my anger so that retaliation can melt into reconciliation. If peace does not begin in my heart, the harshness of war will make every field of life a battleground. Enable me to sow the seeds of peace, to plant a garden of grace, instead.

Jesus: An eye for an eye leaves both you and your enemy blind.

Suggested Scripture:

Matthew 5:1-12
Luke 6:20-26

"YOU ARE THE LIGHT OF THE WORLD . . ."
(MT 5:14).

Jesus, I am becoming more and more aware of the power of light, our dependency upon it, the beauty that only light can express. And now, you tell me that I am light. I feel the burden of those words today. The darkness of my behavior, at times, convicts me of neglect, for then I have hidden the lamp, or worse, not even set flame to its wick.

I long to have the courage of a mountaintop city, but sometimes I fear the heights to which you call me. Chase cowardice from my heart. Fire me with the flame of your light that I might walk boldly into the nights of this world.

Jesus: Fear not the cries you may hear in the darkness; they are brother and sister to your own.

Suggested Scripture:

MATTHEW 5:13-16
MARK 9:50
LUKE 14:34-35

"DO NOT THINK THAT I HAVE COME TO ABOLISH THE LAW OR THE PROPHETS; I HAVE COME NOT TO ABOLISH BUT TO FULFILL" (MT 5:17).

Jesus, there were many times when you appeared to be countercultural to your Jewish brothers. It must have been hard for them to understand your ways. You intended fulfillment, but they saw only destruction—for the Law was their life. How sad that you, the very Word of God, were not taken at your word.

I, too, find it hard to understand your ways at times: to lose is to find, to serve is to lead, to die is to live. Your ways run counter to my deepest instincts. Your road to fullness of life seems to threaten my ideas of survival, and to undermine my natural ambitions. How can I be content with these mysteries? How can I find peace in them as you did?

Jesus: When life no longer requires a solution for you, the mystery will solve itself.

Suggested Scripture:

MATTHEW 5:17-19

> ". . . LEAVE YOUR GIFT THERE BEFORE THE ALTAR AND GO;
> FIRST BE RECONCILED TO YOUR BROTHER OR SISTER, AND
> THEN COME AND OFFER YOUR GIFT"
> **(MT 5:24).**

Jesus, there is no road that leads to God which does not include the companionship of others. I see that clearly now. Were I to go to the altar bearing the guilt of alienation, I would find my brother or sister awaiting me there nonetheless. It is only together with them that I can truly offer my gift—only then would what I had to offer truly be a gift.

You paid the highest price for reconciliation. Clearly, then, I cannot avoid the cost of crossing the bridge that separates me from another. So Jesus, when the span of that bridge reaches farther than my eye can see, give me the strength I need to make a peace-filled crossing.

Jesus: If you cross the bridge of peace, you may see yourself more clearly from the other's side.

Suggested Scripture:

MATTHEW 5:20-25
LUKE 12:57-59

> **"AND IF YOUR RIGHT HAND CAUSES YOU TO SIN, CUT IT OFF AND THROW IT AWAY; IT IS BETTER FOR YOU TO LOSE ONE OF YOUR MEMBERS THAN FOR YOUR WHOLE BODY TO GO INTO HELL"**
> **(MT 5:30).**

These are strong words, Jesus, for a body-conscious age. I cannot imagine losing a limb, much less choosing to cut it off. So the question I must ask myself today is one of values. What is most important to me? Is life eternal really worth the loss of everything else? Does what I look like to others truly say who I am? Perhaps this last is the question I must grapple with.

Surely the gift of my human body was one of the expressions of God's love for me. But am I less valued, less loved, should I no longer be able to walk, talk, see, or hear? Should disease or accident render me dependent and helpless, even maimed, would you turn your back on me and walk away? No, Jesus, I know better than that—you would run to me.

Jesus, you who know my real worth, give me a greater awareness of all that makes me me. Then, let this wholeness lead me to holiness.

Jesus: What I value most is the laughter of your spirit and the love within your heart.

Suggested Scripture:

MATTHEW 5:27-32

A Cup of Grace:

"LET YOUR 'YES' MEAN 'YES,'
AND YOUR 'NO' MEAN 'NO' . . ."
(MT 5:37, NAB).

My prayer is for integrity, Jesus. I catch myself hedging my bets sometimes—not wanting to make definite plans or clear-cut promises. What if something happens to change what my words have set into place? What if I can't fulfill another's need? I don't want to be responsible for someone's disappointment.

Now that I think about all of this, maybe I rely on myself too much and you too little. You place no burdens upon my yes or no; you simply ask that I be clear and honest with my brothers and sisters—that what I say, whatever I say, can be trusted on my word.

Hear my prayer then, Jesus. Place a guard at the door of my lips, not to hold my tongue in fear, but to remind me that the gift of speech is valued treasure.

Jesus: It is only when you lay untruth on the shoulders of your brother or sister that your word becomes a burden.

Suggested Scripture:

MATTHEW 5:33-37

"YOU HAVE HEARD THAT IT WAS SAID, 'AN EYE FOR AN EYE
AND A TOOTH FOR A TOOTH.' BUT I SAY TO YOU, OFFER
NO RESISTANCE TO ONE WHO IS EVIL . . ."
(MT 5:38-39, NAB).

Do not resist someone who has done me evil? But it's so hard not to strike back, Jesus, not to give back the hurt I have received. "Eye and tooth" justice seems so reasonable; I struggle with your words today. My pride pushes against a passivism that might reveal weakness when I feel so strongly justified. Yet once again I hear your call to be more, to go beyond the boundaries of justice to a new, fuller understanding of it. You invite me to nonresistance but not to passivism, and my heart cannot resist you.

I have a choice to make; I will always have a choice. So I need you, Jesus. I need you to help me understand that retaliation would be my sin, not my due.

Jesus: The scales of justice are never held in balance by affliction . . . but by benediction.

Suggested Scripture:

MATTHEW 5:38-42
LUKE 6:29-31

"BUT I SAY TO YOU, LOVE YOUR ENEMIES AND PRAY FOR
THOSE WHO PERSECUTE YOU, SO THAT YOU MAY BE CHIL-
DREN OF YOUR FATHER IN HEAVEN; FOR HE MAKES HIS SUN
RISE ON THE EVIL AND ON THE GOOD . . ."
(MT 5:44-45).

You look into my heart today, Jesus, and call forth a
depth of generosity greater than human expectation. You
seek the hidden corners of my spirit where pain still dwells
and ask me to apply the salve of charity and prayer. I don't
know if I have the courage or the humility to be as indiscriminate as my God; I am more comfortable with condi-
tional love. Your lack of limits and criteria confound my
senses. I cannot comprehend your wide embrace of
mercy, even for me. You see, Jesus, it is not easy to be the
recipient of such a gift—I am not worthy. Help me to
offer healing mercy that I may be healed as well.

Jesus: When you cast compassion upon the earth, you
will see your reflection in the face of your enemy.

Suggested Scripture:

MATTHEW 5:43-48
LUKE 6:27-28, 32-36

"BEWARE OF PRACTICING YOUR PIETY BEFORE OTHERS IN ORDER TO BE SEEN BY THEM . . . YOUR FATHER WHO SEES IN SECRET WILL REWARD YOU"
(MT 6:1-4).

Jesus, time and again, you walk me into the arms of my brothers and sisters on my journey to the kingdom. Today, though, you invite me to secret places—not to hide away but to enter another special relationship—friendship with God. You tell me clearly that your Father-God is not to be exploited, but experienced; that God will be mirrored on faces scrubbed with grace; that the fast that empties me will fill me with your banquet of salvation; that God is to be prayed and praised from the corners of my heart, so that I will speak charity along the streets that I walk; that the alms of a generous life will be a sincere gift only when it is from one who knows compassion and forgiveness.

Jesus, do not let pride bring me to prayer, nor fantasies of holiness to fasting. Give me, instead, simplicity of heart that will lead me to the sanctuary of my soul.

Jesus: Sometimes only closing the door on your *self* opens your heart to others.

Suggested Scripture:

MATTHEW 6:1-6, 16-18

A Cup of Grace:

". . . YOUR FATHER KNOWS WHAT YOU
NEED BEFORE YOU ASK HIM"
(MT 6:8).

Jesus, your words imply such intimacy with God—beyond my comprehension, even my wildest dreams. Yet I draw great comfort and peace, hearing that I am known so well by my God.

Jesus, the daily bread of my life has already been broken in you; I can see why rattling on with a litany of my needs is so unnecessary. But I do think that, when I sit at the banquet table, God is interested in the conversation of my life; so draw me near. Draw me to that place where few words are spoken, yet even whispers are heard. There, let me feast on your love which long was held captive by the needs of my heart.

Jesus: You will always find your voice in the Word.

Suggested Scripture:

MATTHEW 6:7-15
LUKE 11:2-4

"FOR WHERE YOUR TREASURE IS, THERE YOUR HEART WILL BE ALSO" (MT 6:21).

As I grow older, Jesus, directions become unclear. Should I follow the maps of my youth, I fear being marooned on some island of fantasy. Treasure hunts are sometimes hit or miss. When I strike it rich, I want to hold on to the fruit of that good fortune long after it ripens.

Today, you invite me to strike it rich in grace. Then I will never fear. Then, your dreams for me will take reality in my desire for you. The road to riches can begin any-where, can't it, Jesus, for all roads can lead to you. So the kingdom companions me, if I would just look around.

Jesus: Yes, the map you seek is written on your heart.

Suggested Scripture:

MATTHEW 6:19-23
LUKE 12:33-34, 11:34-36

"CAN ANY OF YOU BY WORRYING ADD A SINGLE MOMENT TO YOUR LIFE-SPAN?" (MT 6:27, NAB).

I guess I have some illusion, Jesus, that my worrying will make a difference—that holding on to my concerns will, somehow, keep me and them under control. Yet my anxieties assault my sleep and awaken me with trembling.

Why, Jesus? Why do I see my needs as a burden, when you came to set me free? Why do I retrace my steps, if I know you are the way? Why do I double-check my actions, if your love is my rule of thumb?

Today, free me from the need to be the center of my universe. Open my eyes to see the birds of the air, the flowers of the fields, the good earth that I walk upon. Anoint the scars of my anxieties; then I will no longer value useless worry, but trust in faithful love.

Jesus: The worry that wrinkles your brow may also shrivel your soul.

Suggested Scripture:

MATTHEW 6:24-34
LUKE 12:22-31

"DO NOT JUDGE, SO THAT YOU MAY NOT BE JUDGED" (MT 7:1).

Sometimes I slip, Jesus. I don't mean to. I don't mean to measure another by my rules or standards or ideals. I don't mean to be the drawing board for another's plan of life. To tell the truth, I must admit that even I don't always meet my expectations. Why, then, do I look so critically, examine others so carefully? Why am I not blinded by the beam in my own eye?

Jesus, forgive the glance that too often sees the failure of others. Forgive me my mean measure—my cutting down instead of building up, my cheapness of spirit instead of celebration of soul. Take this self-appointed taskmaster and make, instead, a humble servant.

Jesus: Is that a splinter in your neighbor's eye, or a reflection of the beam in your own?

Suggested Scripture:

MATTHEW 7:1-5
LUKE 6:37-42

A Cup of Grace:

"IN EVERYTHING DO TO OTHERS AS YOU WOULD HAVE
THEM DO TO YOU . . ."
(MT 7:12).

Jesus, if only and always I could remember your words today. If only and always I could be in tune with the instrument of my actions. If only and always the breath of my words was filled with the love of God. If only and always I could bring light and life, compassion and joy. If only and always. . . .

Why? Because, truthfully, I want all these things and more from others, but I know I must first give them. Jesus, how can I give and receive, at the same time, all the goodness you intend for us? How can I be both sides of the same coin, so that I too may be enriched by the treasury of my words and deeds?

Jesus: Let your mind be the home of healing; your lips taste your very words; your heart beat, always, in rhythm with others.

Suggested Scripture:

MATTHEW 7:6, 12-14
LUKE 6:31, 13:23-24

"SO BY THEIR FRUITS YOU WILL KNOW THEM" (MT 7:20, NAB).

Maybe today, Jesus, I should reflect upon my own life and see if others find in me a ripening of good fruit. . . .

Do others find me to be a tree of life? Do I nourish them when they pick the fruit of my words and take them to their hearts? Am I comfort and rest when they lean on me in times of sadness, or depend on me in their fatigue? Is the shade that I provide the shadow of your love? Can others find a home with me, like the birds of the air who make nests in branches? Should I be cut down, would I provide the warmth of a fire . . . or the burden of a cross?

Jesus, draw me to myself that I may taste the fruits of my life, so that "knowing myself as others do" may be fertile soil for this your servant-tree of life.

Jesus: The taproot of God provides taste, touch, and texture for the fruit of your life.

Suggested Scripture:

MATTHEW 7:15-20
LUKE 6:43-45

> "NOT EVERYONE WHO SAYS TO ME, 'LORD, LORD,' WILL
> ENTER THE KINGDOM OF HEAVEN, BUT ONLY THE ONE
> WHO DOES THE WILL OF MY FATHER IN HEAVEN"
> (MT 7:21).

Powerful words, Jesus! As I pray to do the will of God today, I wonder if the words of my prayer are in service of God or of myself. Do my actions wrap my heart's desires as a gift pleasing to your Father-God? Sometimes I fear that only at the end of my life will I come to know the answer. Yet as strong as your words are today, I sense that you do not wish me fear but confidence . . . confidence in you.

So until then, my Jesus, I will rise each day to build my house on rock—on you. The days of castles in the sand are far behind me. Knowing this, I trust that I will recognize the kingdom of heaven, having you as my foundation here on earth.

Jesus: You will build the kingdom by bending your will to form its walls as shelter for the homeless, justice for the voiceless, hope against despair.

Suggested Scripture:

MATTHEW 7:21-29
LUKE 6:46-49, 13:26-27

. . . "LORD, IF YOU CHOOSE, YOU CAN MAKE ME CLEAN."
[JESUS] STRETCHED OUT HIS HAND AND TOUCHED HIM,
SAYING, "I DO CHOOSE. BE MADE CLEAN!"
(MT 8:2-3).

A simple yet direct exchange, Jesus—this leper needed to be touched because no one else would dare; you needed to touch because no one else would care! Today, I am touched by your kindness and chided, somewhat, by this leper's faith in you. He had no doubts. It's as if he could read your heart—the heart of God—and see, clearly, the healing waiting to burst forth.

Jesus, it seems you choose places of alienation. You choose to stand in the chasm created by fear, ignorance, bigotry, and cynicism, so that your outstretched hands can bridge that unholy space and make it whole. I pray you, then, to give me the confidence of this leper, and so invite you to touch those places of alienation I hold within, making them sacred space for your healing grace—because I know you really want to.

Jesus: How could I not stretch out my hand and hallow the hollow? Your flesh is dwelling for the divine.

Suggested Scripture:

MATTHEW 8:1-4
MARK 1:40-45
LUKE 5:12-16

A Cup of Grace:

THE CENTURION ANSWERED, "LORD, I AM NOT WORTHY TO HAVE YOU COME UNDER MY ROOF; BUT ONLY SPEAK THE WORD, AND MY SERVANT WILL BE HEALED"
(MT 8:8).

Once again, Jesus, I am awed by the faith of another. You teach me time and again through friends and family that you desire nothing else but faith, for healing always follows.

Jesus, I am not worthy either. Yet you fashion this reality into an instrument of your love. Should I ask that my unworthiness be healed? How could it ever be? How could I ever be worthy of you, my God! Instead, I pray for the courage, each day, to raise the chalice of my unworthiness to you, then trust the great outpouring of your mercy and love.

Jesus: Unworthiness is not to be resisted. It is a release from struggle and the opportunity for grace.

Suggested Scripture:

MATTHEW 8:5-17
MARK 1:29-34
LUKE 4:38-41, 7:1-10

BUT JESUS SAID TO HIM, "FOLLOW ME, AND LET THE DEAD BURY THE DEAD" (MT 8:22).

Jesus, how hard it is to leave the past behind—the dreams, comforts, hopes, homes, habits, and behaviors, even the failures. Perhaps this last is the hardest. If I am to follow you, though, I must take along only the present and, with this, create the future with you.

The question I raise for myself today is whether or not I can forgive myself as readily and as fully as you do, Jesus. Unforgiveness burdens the journey of life; it deadens my progress and weights my steps. Give me faith in your gift of life, that I may bury the deaths of my past, have the courage to throw off its weight, and the strength of spirit to lighten my own burdens.

Jesus: It is difficult to begin any journey when you believe regret is a necessary companion.

Suggested Scripture:

MATTHEW 8:18-22
LUKE 9:57-62

THEY WERE AMAZED, SAYING, "WHAT SORT OF MAN IS
THIS, THAT EVEN THE WINDS AND THE SEA OBEY HIM?"
(MT 8:27).

If you, the Word of God, brought this earth into being, why wouldn't the winds and sea obey you, Jesus? I wish that I were as obedient. I look at nature and I know that it is not troubled by the Word of God. Effortlessly, it awakens to life, blossoms, fades, and awakens to life once again . . . effortlessly. It is no wonder that I find peace in trees and seas, flowers and sky.

I, on the other hand, strain against the rhythm of my nature; not against the awakening, but the fading. How I wish that my life were effortless!

Jesus: Did you not know that effort *effects* human life?

Suggested Scripture:

MATTHEW 8:23-27
MARK 4:35-41
LUKE 8:22-25

THEN THE WHOLE TOWN CAME OUT TO MEET JESUS; AND WHEN THEY SAW HIM, THEY BEGGED HIM TO LEAVE THEIR NEIGHBORHOOD
(MT 8:34).

We are a funny lot, Jesus—not only do we fear evil, we also fear the good. As you had mercy on the two possessed with demons, have mercy on us today, for we are very much like the people of that town—at least, I know I am.

I believe that each day you want to draw near me. Most days I run to greet you, but there are other days that I know your drawing near will exact a price. It's then that I am like these townsfolk, and beg you to pass by. I have no excuses, Jesus. I do not plead ignorance, because I know in my heart that only good will come. But Jesus, next time you visit, and I am tempted to close the door, please help me to be more hospitable.

Jesus: If you would set your table for guests, I will provide the banquet of salvation.

Suggested Scripture:

MATTHEW 8:28-34
MARK 5:1-20
LUKE 8:26-39

A Cup of Grace:

AND THERE PEOPLE BROUGHT TO [JESUS] A PARALYTIC LYING ON A STRETCHER. WHEN JESUS SAW THEIR FAITH, HE SAID TO THE PARALYTIC, "COURAGE, CHILD, YOUR SINS ARE FORGIVEN"
(MT 9:2, NAB).

Jesus, set me free this day. You know my faith in you; you also know the fears that hold me fast. It is these things that clutter the house of my spirit and tempt my heart to disbelief. Give me the faith of this paralytic, who found freedom in your forgiveness. Let me lean on you for strength. Make me willing to be carried by my need for you, and draw from the wellspring of your compassion.

Your commitment to this paralytic walked him into a dream-come-true. With you as my companion, Jesus, I too will walk unbound into the boundless land of your freedom, for today I hear you say to me, "Courage, child."

Jesus: For each seed, the promise of spring-within is courage enough.

Suggested Scripture:

MATTHEW 9:1-8
MARK 2:1-12
LUKE 5:17-26

AND AS [JESUS] SAT AT DINNER IN THE HOUSE, MANY TAX COLLECTORS AND SINNERS CAME AND WERE SITTING WITH HIM AND HIS DISCIPLES (MT 9:10).

You attracted all kinds of people, Jesus; you must have been quite an enigma to the scribes and Pharisees. Today, still, sinners are drawn to sit at table with you and share the meal of their lives. How non-threatening you must have been; more important, how accepting. I continue to marvel at your openness and compassion, and that such generosity of heart was the cause of your suffering.

Acceptance is one of the greatest gifts I can offer another, yet one of the most difficult to achieve. Oh, I can easily extend generosity of heart from a distance; it is the daily, close-up encounters that present a challenge to me.

Help me not to fear what I do not understand, nor reject a person with whom I disagree. Instead, give me the grace to listen to their stories as you did.

Jesus: The hand of acceptance you extend to another is an embrace of compassion for the sinner in you.

Suggested Scripture:

MATTHEW 9:9-13
MARK 2:13-17
LUKE 5:27-32

A Cup of Grace:

AND JESUS SAID TO THEM, "THE WEDDING GUESTS CAN-
NOT MOURN AS LONG AS THE BRIDEGROOM IS WITH THEM,
CAN THEY? THE DAYS WILL COME WHEN THE BRIDEGROOM
IS TAKEN AWAY FROM THEM, AND THEN THEY WILL FAST"
(MT 9:15).

It is true, Jesus, that loss is always followed by sadness. It seems we lose a part of ourselves when a loved
one leaves us in death. We fast, in a way, as well—our
hearts become a desert; our spirits dry up with longing;
tears become our bread.

Jesus, help me to rejoice and to celebrate each day
with those I love. It is so easy to become distracted by my
own needs. Do not allow me to neglect the gift of their
lives with me, now, so that regret becomes an added burden when you call them home.

Jesus: The presence of your loved ones is the present of
my love.

Suggested Scripture:

MATTHEW 9:14-17
MARK 2:18-22
LUKE 5:33-39

AND WHEN THE DEMON HAD BEEN CAST OUT, THE ONE
WHO HAD BEEN MUTE SPOKE; AND THE CROWDS WERE
AMAZED AND SAID, "NEVER HAS ANYTHING LIKE THIS BEEN
SEEN IN ISRAEL"
(MT 9:33).

Jesus, continue to amaze me—let your grace amaze me. I don't mean, necessarily, that I notice only the extraordinary things that happen around me—those things that wear your disguise of coincidence, those things that enable my heart to see your face.

Amaze me in the disguise of "everyday"—the ordinary, the extraordinary in the ordinary. My day can be so predictable, at times, that I miss your presence in the persons and events that move in and out of my life. Jesus, continue to amaze me today.

Jesus: What seems "in the way" is the way.

Suggested Scripture:

MATTHEW 9:32-38
LUKE 10:2-3

A Cup of Grace:

". . . DO NOT WORRY ABOUT HOW YOU ARE TO SPEAK OR
WHAT YOU ARE TO SAY . . . FOR IT IS NOT YOU WHO SPEAK,
BUT THE SPIRIT . . ."
(MT 10:19-20).

I wish I were less of a worrier, Jesus, but I like to have the answers. I like to know what's coming down the road, what I might need to say and how to say it just right—pressured by the impression I will make.

But I should know better than that. When my life is on the line, my thoughts should be on you, not me. How easy it is to forget you—the Word—the origin of all *my* words. Sometimes I just lose touch with all of that.

Jesus: You are carved on the hand of God. Is that not enough impression for you?

Suggested Scripture:

MATTHEW 10:16-23
MARK 13:9-13
LUKE 21:12-17

"SO DO NOT BE AFRAID; YOU ARE OF MORE VALUE THAN MANY SPARROWS" (MT 10:31).

Then give me the freedom of these birds of the air, Jesus. Let me find myself carried by the winds of your grace. I guess a part of me needs to see the proof of your words, at least sometimes. Forgive me this need and help me find the faith that lives within me.

Teach me how to discover the value that I am for you, so that fear will visit me less and less; so that faith might not be just a guest or kindly visitor, but a truly new life that finds a peaceful dwelling within me.

Jesus: The sparrow does not hesitate to fly, or question the wind for its needs.

Suggested Scripture:

MATTHEW 10:24-33
LUKE 12:2-7

"WHOEVER WELCOMES YOU WELCOMES ME, AND WHOEVER WELCOMES ME WELCOMES THE ONE WHO SENT ME" (MT 10:40).

Jesus, whoever welcomes me, welcomes you? How can you identify yourself with me? Truly, Lord, I am not worthy—I am not worthy of you! And yet, that is not the issue for you because, if it were, this world would never know the presence of God.

Help me to understand that "being" is enough for you; that the disciple can be as the teacher; that creation molded me into the image of God and there we meet as sister and brother—a kinship formed by grace. Jesus, I know this somewhere deep in my heart; help me.

Jesus: The dust of the earth—your flesh—was kissed by the breath of God.

Suggested Scripture:

MATTHEW 10:34–11:1
MARK 9:41
LUKE 12:51-53, 14:26-27

**"WOE TO YOU, CHORAZIN! WOE TO YOU, BETHSAIDA!
FOR IF THE DEEDS OF POWER DONE IN YOU HAD BEEN
DONE IN TYRE AND SIDON, THEY WOULD HAVE REPENTED
LONG AGO IN SACKCLOTH AND ASHES"
(MT 11:21).**

I, too, have been like Chorazin and Bethsaida, Jesus, when I forget the deeds of power you have worked in my life. I have experienced so many resurrections that have been wrought by your grace. I have been saved time and again by your dying; yet there are still so many times I forget your life within me—a life that has changed and continues to change the course of mine. Forgive this night within me that blinds my heart from remembering. Never stop calling me to the conversion each day can bring.

Jesus: When you take a walk into your heart, the gift of remembering is found.

Suggested Scripture:

MATTHEW 11:20-24
LUKE 10:13-15

A Cup of Grace:

Jesus, thank you for this reminder; I know I do not thank God enough. Why? I think I get too focused on my needs, and the needs of those I love, so that I lose sight of the whole picture of my life. The forest of your myriad grace is lost by the trees of routine I pass along the way. Yet a part of me does know that what appear to be roadblocks in my life are also opportunities for your grace. I should be thankful in all things, then, but I'm not.

Jesus, while this deeper truth finds its way to my faith in you, open my child-eyes so that I will give thanks more often for the blessings all around me.

Jesus: What is lost to your eyes is found in God's vision.

Suggested Scripture:

MATTHEW 11:25-27
LUKE 10:21-22

"FOR MY YOKE IS EASY, AND MY BURDEN IS LIGHT" (MT 11:30).

Jesus, how can that be? How can any burden be light—especially yours? Yes, I would come to you readily to find comfort and peace, but to shoulder your yoke and carry your burden would only sink me deeper into the mire of my own difficulties—wouldn't it? How can you lighten my burden with yours, and make easy the yoke of my life?

Jesus: When I wore the yoke of the cross, you were no burden to me.

Suggested Scripture:

MATTHEW 11:28-30

BUT THE PHARISEES WENT OUT AND CONSPIRED AGAINST [JESUS], HOW TO DESTROY HIM. WHEN JESUS BECAME AWARE OF THIS, HE DEPARTED (MT 12:14-15).

You were not one to pick a fight, Jesus, or stay where you were not welcome. There are times in my life when moving on is wiser than staying—wiser and healthier—but sometimes I hang on instead. I don't like to "give in" or give up. It's then I dig in my heels and my heart, refusing to let go. Unlike you, my life is not in the balance, but I act like it is. There is a time for all things and when that time is over, it is over—but it's so hard for me to let go.

Jesus: The embrace of God awaits those who let go.

Suggested Scripture:

MATTHEW 12:14-21

"AGAIN, THE KINGDOM OF HEAVEN IS LIKE A NET THROWN
INTO THE SEA, WHICH COLLECTS FISH OF EVERY KIND.
WHEN IT IS FULL THEY . . . PUT WHAT IS GOOD INTO
BUCKETS. WHAT IS BAD THEY THROW AWAY"
(MT 13:47-48, NAB).

Jesus, the kingdom of heaven embraces the sea of my
life. There are times when my net is full, and I must sit
down and sort out the good and the not-so-good collect-
ed along the way. Life is like that—coming to a point,
now and then, of sorting out.

As I grow older, I am less inclined to mark clear-cut
lines between good and bad. I'm more inclined to balance
my scale with the weight of grace; only then can I take
true measure of my experience. Is this the weight of your
wisdom, Jesus, or should I be more discriminating?

Jesus: Grace achieves balance when experience cannot.

Suggested Scripture:

MATTHEW 13:47-53

A Cup of Grace:

**"TRULY I TELL YOU, WHATEVER YOU BIND ON EARTH WILL
BE BOUND IN HEAVEN, AND WHATEVER YOU LOOSE ON
EARTH WILL BE LOOSED IN HEAVEN"
(MT 18:18).**

Binding and loosing are the responsibilities of your disciples, Jesus—so they are mine as well. Not that I think that what I do reaches the heights of heaven, but I certainly make an impact in my place on this earth.

I can bind or loose another with my words and actions; I know that. Let gentleness precede me, then, in my relationships because the kind of "binding" I might do can stifle, not bring fulfillment—the fullness of life that you brought us. And when I "loose," may it be with hands that bless in true freedom—the free gift of you.

Jesus: Each time you bind another, you keep yourself from freedom.

Suggested Scripture:

MATTHEW 18:15-20

"... 'THESE LAST WORKED ONLY ONE HOUR, AND YOU
HAVE MADE THEM EQUAL TO US WHO HAVE BORNE THE
BURDEN OF THE DAY AND THE SCORCHING HEAT'"
(MT 20:12).

Why do I do what I do, Jesus? Is it for a reward—the final reward, heaven? Or is it because I believe the doing, itself, is a value? What is my goal? What is my motive? Are you my "staying power" for a job well done?

So many questions are raised for me today, Jesus; for these I am grateful. Help me to be honest with myself when I find the answers. Keep jealousy from my heart and comparison from my lips as I pursue the daily round of my life. At the end, I want to greet my generous God with a smile.

Jesus: God only perplexes those who think they have no equal.

Suggested Scripture:

MATTHEW 20:1-16

"WOE TO YOU, SCRIBES AND PHARISEES, HYPOCRITES! FOR YOU CLEAN THE OUTSIDE OF THE CUP AND OF THE PLATE, BUT INSIDE THEY ARE FULL OF GREED AND SELF-INDULGENCE"
(MT 23:25).

Forgive me, Jesus, when the scribe and Pharisee within me pay too much attention to the "look" of things. I try to stay true to their truth, but I don't always succeed. I get caught up in what I see, still missing the greater picture—the spirit who lives within. Not that straightening things out and getting them in order is wrong, but I sometimes do violence to the person within—myself and others.

When I want to "clean house" in the future, Jesus, don't let me be content with a few coats of paint on the outside. Remind me to open the doors of my home and look within. Only then will I become hospitality to myself and my neighbors.

Jesus: It is what the cup holds that makes it a chalice.

Suggested Scripture:

MATTHEW 23:23-26

"KEEP AWAKE THEREFORE, FOR YOU KNOW NEITHER THE DAY NOR THE HOUR"
(MT 25:13).

At first hearing, these words of yours feel quite threatening—a warning that sounds alarm within me. Will I be ready for my God? Is worry your legacy to us—to me—this day?

Keep awake! Be ready! Double-check! This is no way to live, Jesus, if it keeps me from really living. Is this the way to the kingdom? How do I keep vigil, yet go about my daily routine—when the days are too busy to concentrate on too much?

I will take your words today as the confidence of a friend, rather than fear their meaning. You are the way to the kingdom, Jesus. So with my eyes on you, I will be prepared to cross the threshold of this life into God's fullness. Keep me focused, Jesus—keep me focused.

Jesus: Awake or asleep, the eyes of a pilgrim-heart see rightly.

Suggested Scripture:

MATTHEW 25:1-13

HE WAS HIS MOTHER'S ONLY SON,
AND SHE WAS A WIDOW . . .
(Lk 7:12).

Jesus, seeing the widow of Nain come toward you, weeping at the death of her son, were you reminded of your own mother? Did your heart know that she would shed tears one day . . . tears over you? Were you filled with compassion, as the gospel tells us, because you identified so deeply, so fully?

With all your miracles, words, and good works, I sometimes forget that your heart went into all your love and healing, your feelings, your "knowing." Your heart moved you to be moved. Help me to be as sensitive as you, for you touch me once again today.

Jesus: Compassion is heart-wisdom.

Suggested Scripture:

Luke 7:11-17

... "IF [JESUS] WERE A PROPHET, HE WOULD HAVE
KNOWN WHO AND WHAT KIND OF WOMAN THIS IS WHO IS
TOUCHING HIM—THAT SHE IS A SINNER"
(LK 7:39).

Patience again, Jesus. People were always testing you, looking for flaws, for proof. Proof against you. They just didn't "get it," and chose to condemn generous compassion and forgiveness to death.

Do I do that to you, Jesus? Am I, too, cynical of your unconditional love at times? Do I try to limit the abundant life that you offer me? If I do, it does not matter, I know, because you do not permit anything to keep you from me. As I touch you in my prayer, you touch me in forgiveness. You let nothing hold me from your good wishes of forgiving love.

Today I thank God for you and the example of your boundless understanding and courageous, tender love.

Jesus: Sinners recognize sinners. I see the image of God.

Suggested Scripture:

LUKE 7:36-50

SOON AFTERWARDS [JESUS] WENT ON THROUGH CITIES
AND VILLAGES . . . BRINGING THE GOOD NEWS. . . . THE
TWELVE WERE WITH HIM, AS WELL AS SOME WOMEN . . .
WHO PROVIDED FOR THEM OUT OF THEIR RESOURCES
(LK 8:1-3).

Those whose lives you touched could not help but want to follow you, Jesus. Today, we might call these women the unsung heroines of the gospel. Giving up their lives of home and friendship, they sought to further your teaching and good works by their presence and assistance. Magdalene, Joanna, Susanna—women cured and set free to live freely—chose to provide for you and your disciples instead of going their own way, but so little is said about them, so little written except that they were there.

Help me to appreciate the unsung people of my day and my life—the people around me who work and sacrifice in quiet ways, who get little notice and little note. Help me to become aware of the "extras" I take for granted, of the work others do to make my work easier.

Jesus: Looking beyond yourself is a seed of contemplation.

Suggested Scripture:

LUKE 8:1-3

... BUT [THE SAMARITANS] DID NOT RECEIVE [JESUS]. . . . [JAMES AND JOHN] SAID, "LORD, DO YOU WANT US TO COMMAND FIRE TO COME DOWN FROM HEAVEN AND CON-SUME THEM? BUT [JESUS] TURNED AND REBUKED THEM (LK 9:53-55).

Jesus, you never force yourself upon me; neither do you punish me for my lack of faith—for all those times you have been present in my life, but I could not see. I want to have that respect for others. I want to do unto them as you have done unto me.

When I am not "received" by others, turned away by them for my thoughts or ideas, help me not to reject them in return. Let retribution be a foreign land where my heart does not choose to travel. Jesus, help me to move on, not hold on.

Jesus: Making another "pay" leaves you poor.

Suggested Scripture:

LUKE 9:51-56

"GO ON YOUR WAY; BEHOLD, I AM SENDING YOU LIKE LAMBS AMONG WOLVES" (LK 10:3, NAB).

Like lambs among wolves. . . . Was your way of life so starkly in contrast to the society of your day, Jesus? Your words seem to tell me so. Today, is that way of life of equal contrast? Perhaps it is and I have not paid close attention. Yes, I read the papers and watch the news, and shake my head at the death and violence there; but do I live like a lamb among wolves? Do I put my life on the line with my prayers? Do I act on peace and justice, or do I leave it to somebody else? Do I have the simplicity of a lamb, or am I just wearing sheep's clothing?

Jesus, you send me out each day; give me, then, the courage and urgency of your disciples.

Jesus: The courage of the lamb is in following the Shepherd.

Suggested Scripture:

LUKE 10:1-12

**[JESUS ASKED], "WHICH OF THESE THREE, IN YOUR OPIN-
ION, WAS A NEIGHBOR TO THE ROBBERS' VICTIM?" [THE
LAWYER] ANSWERED, "THE ONE WHO TREATED HIM WITH
MERCY." JESUS SAID TO HIM, "GO AND DO LIKEWISE"
(LK 10:36-37, NAB).**

Mercy springs from love—that is what I hear you tell
me today, Jesus. When I look at my own life, that has
been your greatest gift to me. Your gentleness, acceptance, even tenderness has been a lived and tangible experience of your love for me.

Thank you for the wideness of your mercy. It has
helped me become comfortable with the "all of me"—
light and shadow. Now, it's my turn; changed by you, help
me live this change-reaction of merciful love. Make me
sensitive to those moments when gentle acceptance, forgiveness, caring beyond expectations is what is asked of
me—creating the bridge to others that you built, over and
over again, to me. My Jesus . . . mercy.

Jesus: Mercy given is mercy received.

Suggested Scripture:

MATTHEW 22:34-40
MARK 12:28-34
LUKE 10:25-37

[MARTHA] HAD A SISTER NAMED MARY, WHO SAT AT THE
LORD'S FEET AND LISTENED TO WHAT HE WAS SAYING.
BUT MARTHA WAS DISTRACTED BY HER MANY TASKS . . .
(LK 10:39-40).

How much like Martha I am, Jesus—so easily distracted by many things. Mary knew how to pay attention—that's what strikes me so clearly today.

When people come to the door of my day, seeking hospitality, do I pay attention? Not all the time. Yes, I listen, but with only one ear—I also hear the cries of the task at hand, and they pull me close; I doubt that I listen at all with my heart. It's that inner hearing that others seek; it's also what I seek from others.

Jesus, when anyone comes to me again, seeking my company, remind me of the privilege of that visit and call to my heart as they do.

Jesus: To hold another's heart is to be held by theirs.

Suggested Scripture:

LUKE 10:38-42

"BUT GOD SAID TO HIM, 'YOU FOOL! THIS VERY NIGHT YOUR LIFE IS BEING DEMANDED OF YOU. AND THE THINGS YOU HAVE PREPARED, WHOSE WILL THEY BE?' SO IT IS WITH THOSE WHO STORE UP TREASURES FOR THEMSELVES BUT ARE NOT RICH TOWARD GOD"

(LK 12:20-21).

I, too, have been blessed with abundance, Jesus—make me grateful in all things. Give me the freedom to share what I have, and to know that what I have is only and always the gift of God. May God be my point of reference, and stewardship the pivot of my turning.

Jesus, you call me friend; with you and in you, I want to place the riches of my life into the hands of our provident God. I may not have barns in which to store these blessings, but keep me generous nonetheless, generous, with a hand always open and a heart ever-mindful of my greatest gift . . . you.

Jesus: Humility holds you to holy ground.

Suggested Scripture:

LUKE 12:13-21

A Cup of Grace:

"[THE GARDENER] REPLIED, 'SIR, LET [THE FIG TREE]
ALONE FOR ONE MORE YEAR, UNTIL I DIG AROUND IT AND
PUT MANURE ON IT. IF IT BEARS FRUIT NEXT YEAR, WELL
AND GOOD; BUT IF NOT, YOU CAN CUT IT DOWN'"
(LK 13:8-9).

There's always hope for me too, Jesus. The Divine Gardener constantly reaches down and cultivates the soil of my life, long after my planting on this earth. Rooted in you, Jesus, I am held firm and continue to reach for the bright light of your life. Some of my seasons have not been as fertile as others, but you see me through those times—nourishing the ground of my being with grace.

Let me hold fast to you through the coming autumns and winters of my life, so that I may bear fruit in the summer of the kingdom—for the garden of which I am part on this earth reaches into that season of new life.

Jesus: Grace seasons life.

Suggested Scripture:

LUKE 13:1-9

BUT THE LEADER OF THE SYNAGOGUE, INDIGNANT
BECAUSE JESUS HAD CURED ON THE SABBATH, KEPT SAY-
ING TO THE CROWD, "THERE ARE SIX DAYS ON WHICH
WORK OUGHT TO BE DONE; COME ON THOSE DAYS
AND BE CURED . . ."

(LK 13:14).

The leader of the synagogue is ungrateful for your work of love, Jesus. He is caught in a rigid perspective of the spiritual life—foolishly thinking he can limit spontaneous grace. Love follows no schedule, and neither does healing.

Today I wonder if I ever put you on a timetable. Do I expect your love and healing at certain times, in specific ways, in those places that I have formulated for you? I know you love and heal me in spite of myself; but it sometimes takes longer for me to discover how I have been blessed.

Jesus, you never claimed to be a tidy package—the Spirit blows where it will, and surprise can be God in disguise. Do not let me be frightened or ungrateful each time you sweep grace through the settled spaces of my heart.

Jesus: When you box me in, you are left outside.

Suggested Scripture:

LUKE 13:10-17

Anita M. Constance, SC

is director of pastoral care at Saint Anne Villa in Convent Station, New Jersey. Her work has included ministry with senior citizens as well as ministry in bereavement, liturgy, spiritual direction, and pastoral counseling. Her previous books include *Night Vision . . . Praying Through Change*, *A Time to Turn . . . The Paschal Experience*, and *Advent Thirst . . . Christmas Hope* (Paulist Press). She is also editor of *Living the Days of Lent*, an annual publication of Paulist Press.